P9-CCW-154

Crisco. Year-Round Holiday Magic

Publications International, Ltd.

Favorite Brand Name Recipes at www.fbnr.com

Copyright © 2004 Publications International, Ltd.

Recipes and text © 2004 The J.M. Smucker company.
All photographs © Publications International except those on pages 80, 81
and 87 © The J.M. Smucker Company
All rights reserved. This publication may not be reproduced or quoted in whole or
in part by any means whatsoever without written permission from:

Louis Weber, CEO
Publications International, Ltd.
7373 North Cicero Avenue
Lincolnwood, IL 60712

Permission is never granted for commercial purposes.

Some of the products listed in this publication may be in limited distribution.

Jif®, Smucker's® and CRISCO® are trademarks of The J.M. Smucker Company.

Front and back cover photography and photography on pages 9, 11, 15, 19, 21, 23,
25, 27, 29, 31, 33, 35, 39, 41, 45, 51, 55, 56, 59, 61, 63, 65, 66, 67 and 70 by
Stephen Hamilton Photographics, Inc., Chicago
Photographer: Tate Hunt
Food Stylist: Susie Skoog
Prop Stylist: Paula Walters

Pictured on the front cover *(clockwise from upper left)***:** Raspberry Linzer
Rounds *(page 52)*, Peppermint Cookies *(page 50)* and Classic Sugar Cookies
(page 56).

Pictured on the back cover *(counterclockwise from top):* Easter Bunny Cake
(page 78), All-American Apple Pie *(page 18)* and Vanilla Chocolate Swirl Ice
Cream Cone Cakes *(page 8).*

ISBN: 1-4127-2036-2

Manufactured in China.

8 7 6 5 4 3 2 1

Microwave Cooking: Microwave ovens vary in wattage. Use the cooking times as
guidelines and check for doneness before adding more time.

Contents

30

60

28

Celebrations Around the Calendar

The holiday season is filled with family meals and celebrations with friends—but as we all know, special occasions occur throughout the year. That's why we've created *Year-Round Holiday Magic*: because a birthday, holiday, or festive gathering is always just around the corner, and there's no better way to enjoy it than by sharing a meal or a treat with our loved ones.

CRISCO® recipes—easy and delicious—are perfect for every special occasion. Dad will love the Father's Day Tie Cookie as part of a delicious brunch menu, and Mom will appreciate the Cherry Nut Coffee Cake you'll find among the dishes for a Mother's Day Tea Time. Whether it's St. Patrick's Day, Cinco de Mayo, Halloween, New Year's Eve, or just a Super Bowl party, *Year-Round Holiday Magic* has the quick, simple recipes that you'll need when getting together with family and friends.

Here are a few storage tips to help you keep baked goods fresh longer—or to help you prepare foods ahead of time, and then reheat and serve at the last minute:

Cookies and Bars

Unbaked cookie dough can be refrigerated for up to one week or frozen for up to six weeks. Rolls of dough (for slice-and-bake cookies) should be sealed tightly in plastic wrap; other doughs should be stored in airtight containers. For convenience, label plastic wrap or container with baking information.

Store soft and crisp cookies separately at room temperature to prevent changes in texture and flavor. Keep soft cookies in airtight containers. If they begin to dry out, add a piece of apple or a slice of bread to the container to help them retain moisture. Store crisp cookies in containers with loose-fitting lids to prevent moisture buildup. Store cookies with sticky glazes, fragile decorations, and icings in single layers between sheets of waxed paper.

As a rule, crisp cookies freeze better than soft, moist cookies. However, rich, buttery bar cookies are an exception because they freeze extremely well. Freeze baked cookies in airtight containers or freezer bags for up to six months. Thaw cookies and brownies unwrapped at room temperature.

Cakes

Store one-layer frosted cakes in their baking pans, tightly covered. Store layered frosted cakes under a cake cover or under a large inverted bowl. Cakes with whipped cream frostings or cream fillings should always be stored in the refrigerator.

Unfrosted cakes can be frozen up to four months if well-wrapped in plastic wrap. Thaw them, unwrapped, at room temperature. Frosted cakes should be frozen unwrapped until the frosting hardens, and then wrapped, sealed, and frozen for up to two months. To thaw, remove the wrapping and thaw at room temperature or in the refrigerator. Cakes with fruit or custard fillings don't freeze well because they become soggy when thawed.

Breads and Muffins

Quick breads should be wrapped well in plastic wrap and stored at room temperature to stay fresh up to one week. Or, they may be frozen for up to three months wrapped in heavy-duty foil. Muffins should be stored in a sealed plastic food storage bag up to three days. Or, they may be frozen for up to one month wrapped in heavy-duty foil.

Pies

Unbaked pie dough can be frozen for later use. Simply flatten the dough into disks and stack in a freezer bag with waxed paper between the layers.

Meringue-topped pies are best when served the day they are made; leftovers should be refrigerated. Custard or cream pies should be refrigerated immediately after cooling. Fruit pies should be covered and stored at room temperature overnight; refrigerate them for longer storage.

To freeze unbaked fruit pies, do not cut steam vents in the top crust. Cover them with inverted paper plates for extra protection and package in freezer bags or plastic wrap. To bake, do not thaw. Cut slits in the top crust and allow an additional 15 to 20 minutes of baking time. Baked fruit pies can be frozen after they're completely cooled. To serve, let the pie thaw at room temperature for two hours, then heat until warm. Pies with cream or custard fillings and meringue toppings don't freeze well.

Vanilla Chocolate Swirl Ice Cream Cone Cakes

MAKES 12 CONE CAKES

¼ CRISCO® Stick or ¼ cup CRISCO Shortening

¾ cup sugar

1 egg, slightly beaten

½ teaspoon vanilla

1 cup sifted cake flour

1 teaspoon baking powder

⅛ teaspoon salt

¼ cup milk

2 tablespoons cocoa powder

2 tablespoons mini chocolate chips

12 large flat-bottom ice cream cones

Buttery Cream Frosting (recipe on page 78)

Preheat oven to 350°F.

Beat CRISCO Shortening and sugar vigorously by hand or at medium speed with electric mixer for 2 minutes. Add egg and vanilla; mix well.

Combine cake flour, baking powder and salt. Add to CRISCO mixture alternately with milk, mixing thoroughly after each addition. Place half the batter in a separate bowl and stir in cocoa and mini chocolate chips. Mix with wooden spoon until well blended.

Divide the batters into cones, alternating chocolate and plain batter. Run a skewer through the batter once or twice to "swirl" the colors. Set cones in muffin cups or on a baking sheet. Bake for 25 to 30 minutes; cool.

Prepare Buttery Cream Frosting and frost cakes, or pipe on the frosting with a star tip in a circular pattern to create a "swirled" top. Decorate with assorted candies, sprinkles, coconut and marshmallows; top with a maraschino cherry.

Birthdays

Double Decadence Chocolate Cake with Shiny Chocolate Icing

MAKES 12 SERVINGS

Double Decadence Chocolate Cake

- ½ cup semisweet chocolate chips
- 1½ cups hot coffee
- 3 cups sugar
- 2½ cups all-purpose flour
- 1½ cups unsweetened cocoa powder
- 2 teaspoons baking soda
- ¾ teaspoon baking powder
- 1¼ teaspoons salt
- 3 eggs
- ¾ cup CRISCO® Oil
- 1½ cups buttermilk
- 1 teaspoon vanilla

Shiny Chocolate Icing

- 1 cup heavy cream
- 2 tablespoons sugar
- 2 tablespoons light corn syrup
- 2 cups semisweet chocolate chips
- ¼ Butter Flavor CRISCO Stick or ¼ cup Butter Flavor CRISCO Shortening

Double Decadence Chocolate Cake

Preheat oven to 300°F.

Spray 2 (9-inch) round cake pans with CRISCO No-Stick Cooking Spray. Line bottoms with rounds of waxed paper or parchment paper and spray again.

Combine chocolate chips and coffee in a bowl. Let mixture stand, whisking occasionally, until chocolate is melted and mixture is smooth.

Whisk together sugar, flour, cocoa, baking soda, baking powder and salt in a large bowl.

Beat eggs with an electric mixer at high speed 3 to 5 minutes or until thick. Slowly add CRISCO Oil, buttermilk, vanilla and melted chocolate mixture to eggs, beating until well combined. Add dry ingredients and beat on medium speed until just combined.

Divide batter between pans and bake in middle of oven 45 to 55 minutes or until a toothpick inserted in center comes out clean. Cool layers

Birthdays

in pans on racks for 30 to 45 minutes. Run a thin knife around edges of pans and invert layers onto racks. Carefully remove waxed paper and cool layers completely.

Shiny Chocolate Icing
In a 1½- to 2-quart saucepan, whisk together the cream, sugar and corn syrup. Bring to a boil over medium heat, whisking until sugar is dissolved. Remove pan from heat and add chocolate chips, whisking until chocolate is melted and mixture is smooth. Cut CRISCO Shortening into 3 pieces and add to frosting, whisking until smooth.

Transfer icing to a bowl and chill until spreadable, about 30 minutes. Spread icing between cake layers and over top and sides.

Note: If covered and chilled, cake will keep for 3 days. Bring cake to room temperature before serving.

Birthdays

Classic Yellow Cake

MAKES 1 (8-INCH) OR (9-INCH) CAKE

2 (8-inch) layers

2 cups sifted cake flour

1⅓ cups sugar

3 teaspoons baking powder

1 teaspoon salt

½ CRISCO® Stick or ½ cup CRISCO Shortening

1 cup milk, divided

2 eggs

1 teaspoon vanilla

2 (9-inch) layers

2½ cups sifted cake flour

1⅔ cups sugar

3½ teaspoons baking powder

1 teaspoon salt

⅔ CRISCO Stick or ⅔ cup CRISCO Shortening

1¼ cups milk, divided

3 eggs

1 teaspoon vanilla

Preheat oven to 350°F.

Spray 2 (8-or 9-inch) cake pans with CRISCO No-Stick Cooking Spray and dust with flour.

Combine flour, sugar, baking powder and salt in mixing bowl. Add CRISCO Shortening and ⅔ cup milk (¾ cup for 9-inch pan). Beat at medium speed of electric mixer for 2 minutes.

Add eggs, the remaining milk and vanilla. Beat for 2 minutes. Pour into prepared pans.

Bake 8-inch layers about 30 minutes and 9-inch layers about 40 minutes or until a toothpick inserted into the center comes out clean.

Cool for 10 to 15 minutes on wire racks. Remove from pans; cool completely. Frost as desired.

Variations

Almond Tea Cakes: Substitute 1 teaspoon almond flavoring for vanilla. Half fill muffin pans that have been sprayed with CRISCO No-Stick Cooking Spray or lined with paper liners. Sprinkle with confectioners' sugar and chopped almonds. Bake at 375°F about 15 minutes. Makes about 2 dozen cupcakes.

Coconut Flake Cake: Substitute ½ teaspoon almond flavoring and ½ teaspoon vanilla. Stir 1⅓ cups flaked coconut (3½-ounce can) into cake batter.

Silly Birthday Party

Fool around at the silliest birthday party!

Invite all your friends to the silliest party around. You can make invitations by looking in a mirror and writing everything backward. (You might want to write a hint in regular writing that lets your guests know that they need a mirror to read their invitations!) Ask everyone to wear funny outfits, like a striped shirt with polka-dotted or plaid pants, mismatched socks, and a funny hat. When they ring the front doorbell, walk backward and greet them by saying "Goodbye!" instead of "Hello." Serve your guests inside-out sandwiches (a cracker between two pieces of cheese). Later, have a silly stunt contest. To hold the contest, ask guests to do silly things, such as walk backward on their knees while holding their ankles behind them or balancing a penny on their noses while walking across the room.

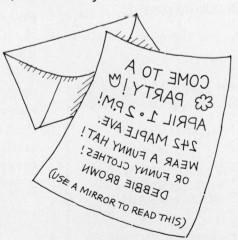

Best Cherry Pie

MAKES ONE 9-INCH PIE

1 unbaked Classic
   CRISCO® Double
   Pie Crust*
¾ cup sugar
3 tablespoons flour
⅛ teaspoon salt
¼ cup cherry juice
   Few drops red food
   coloring (optional)
2 cans (16 ounces each)
   red sour pitted cher-
   ries, drained
1 tablespoon butter
   or margarine
½ teaspoon almond
   extract (optional)
¼ cup half-and-half
1 egg, lightly beaten

Recipe on page 16

Prepare pie crust; set aside.

Preheat oven to 400°F.

Combine sugar, flour and salt in a medium saucepan. Whisk in cherry juice and red food coloring, if desired; add cherries.

Cook and stir over medium heat until mixture has boiled 1 minute. Remove from heat; stir in butter and almond extract, if desired.

Pour filling into unbaked pie crust. Roll out top crust. Using a 1½-inch star cutter, cut 3 stars in the center of the crust. Place top crust over filling; trim and seal. Roll out leftover scraps to ⅛-inch thickness and cut into star garnishes. Place on crust as desired.

Whisk together half-and-half and egg. Brush top crust and garnish with egg wash. Bake for about 30 minutes or until golden brown.

4th of July • Memorial Day

SHISH KABOBS
•
GRILLED PORTOBELLO
MUSHROOMS AND
SUMMER SQUASH
•
DILLED POTATO SALAD
•
ALL-AMERICAN PIES

Summer

Classic CRISCO® Pie Crust

Single Crust

1⅓ cups all-purpose flour

½ teaspoon salt

½ CRISCO Stick or ½ cup CRISCO Shortening

3 tablespoons cold water

Double Crust

2 cups all-purpose flour

1 teaspoon salt

¾ CRISCO Stick or ¾ cup CRISCO Shortening

5 tablespoons cold water

1 (9-inch) Deep Dish Double Crust or 2 (10-inch) Double Crust

2⅔ cups all-purpose flour

1 teaspoon salt

1 CRISCO Stick or 1 cup CRISCO Shortening

7 to 8 tablespoons cold water

Spoon flour into measuring cup and level. Mix flour and salt in medium bowl. Cut in CRISCO Shortening using pastry blender (or 2 knives) until all flour is blended in to form pea-size chunks. Sprinkle with water, 1 tablespoon at a time. Toss lightly with fork until dough forms a ball.

Divide dough in half if making double crust. Press between hands to form 1 or 2 (5- to 6-inch) pancakes. Lightly flour dough. Roll into circle.

For single crust, transfer dough to pie plate using rolling pin. Press dough to fit. Fold edge under. Flute.

1 *Cut CRISCO® Shortening into flour*

2 *Press dough between hands*

3 *Roll out dough ⅛-inch thick*

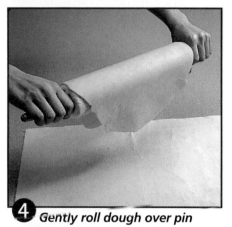

4 *Gently roll dough over pin*

For double crust, lightly flour each half of dough. Roll into circles. Transfer bottom crust to pie plate using rolling pin. Press dough to fit. Trim edge even with pie plate. Add desired filling to unbaked pie crust. Lift top crust onto filled pie. Trim to ½-inch beyond edge of pie plate. Fold top edge under bottom crust. Flute. Cut slits in top crust to allow steam to escape. Bake according to specific recipe instructions.

For single baked pie shell, preheat oven to 425°F. Thoroughly prick bottom and sides with fork (50 times) to prevent shrinking. Bake for 10 to 15 minutes or until lightly browned.

For recipe calling for unbaked pie shell, bake according to specific recipe instructions.

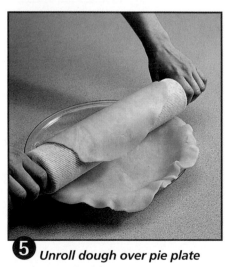

5 *Unroll dough over pie plate*

Summer

All-American Apple Pie

MAKES 1 (9-INCH) PIE

- **1 unbaked Classic CRISCO® Double Pie Crust***
- **6 medium cooking apples**
- **¾ cup sugar**
- **2 tablespoons all-purpose flour**
- **1 teaspoon cinnamon**
- **1 tablespoon butter or margarine**
- **1 egg white, lightly beaten**

Garnish

- **1 unbaked Classic CRISCO Single Pie Crust***

***Recipe on page 16**

Preheat oven to 400°F.

Prepare pie crust; set aside.

For filling, pare, core and slice apples; toss with mixture of sugar, flour and cinnamon. Pour into unbaked pie crust; dot with butter.

Cover with top crust; seal and flute edge. Brush with egg white. Cut slits for steam to escape.

Roll additional crust to ⅛-inch-thickness. With small 1½-inch star cookie cutter, cut 20 to 25 stars. Place 1 star on rim of top crust; brush with egg glaze. Repeat until rim is covered.

Bake for 30 to 40 minutes, until pie is golden brown and apples are tender.

All About Apples

There are many types of apples. Be sure to use the variety that's best for the job:

For pies: Granny Smith, Golden Delicious, Red Delicious, Jonathan, Pippin, York Imperial

For baking whole: Jonathan, Northern Spy, York Imperial, Baldwin, Golden Delicious, Red Delicious

For applesauce: McIntosh, Red Delicious, Golden Delicious, Rome Beauty

To core an apple, slice it in half lengthwise. Remove the center core with the larger end of a melon baller.

Patriotic Berry Pie

MAKES 1 (9-INCH) PIE

1 (9-inch) baked Classic CRISCO® Single Pie Crust*

1⅔ cups sugar, divided

1 cup all-purpose flour

1½ cups half-and-half

2 eggs

1 teaspoon vanilla

1½ cups fresh blueberries

2 tablespoons cornstarch

2 tablespoons strawberry gelatin

⅔ cup water

3 pints fresh strawberries

Mint sprigs for garnish

Recipe on page 16

Prepare pie crust; set aside.

Combine 1 cup sugar and flour in a heavy saucepan; whisk in half-and-half and eggs. Bring to a boil over medium heat, whisking constantly; boil 1 minute or until thickened. Add vanilla; cool.

Spoon custard mixture into baked pie crust. Arrange blueberries over custard mixture.

Combine remaining ⅔ cup sugar, cornstarch and gelatin in a saucepan. Gradually stir in water. Bring to a boil, stirring constantly; boil 1 minute. Pour half the mixture over the blueberries. Chill 30 minutes or until set.

Arrange strawberries over blueberries, pointed-end up. Drizzle with remaining gelatin mixture. Chill until set. Garnish with mint sprigs.

In Season

Blueberries are in season in late summer. They're delicious fresh, and are wonderful in baked goods, sprinkled over cereal and ice cream, and eaten by the handful.

Blueberries are an excellent source of vitamin C and fiber. They freeze beautifully and are a welcome reminder of warmer days if you save them for the dreary days of winter.

Choose berries that are plump, firm and uniformly colored. Avoid berries that are withered.

Check out our website, **www.crisco.com,** for more blueberry recipes, including: *Blueberry Orange Muffins, Blueberry Pie and Blueberry Bread.*

Shish Kabobs

MAKES ABOUT 8 SERVINGS

½ cup CRISCO® Oil

½ cup chopped onion

¼ cup red wine vinegar

¼ cup ketchup

2 tablespoons Worcestershire sauce

2 cloves garlic, peeled and mashed

1 teaspoon salt

½ teaspoon chopped fresh oregano or rosemary

¼ teaspoon pepper

3 pounds lamb or beef, cut into 1-inch cubes

Green pepper squares

Small onions

Tomato wedges or cherry tomatoes

Mushrooms

Combine first 9 ingredients in a large bowl. Add meat and stir to coat with sauce. Cover and refrigerate overnight.

Alternately skewer cubes of meat with desired combination of green pepper squares, small onions, tomatoes and mushrooms.

Preheat broiler. Place kabobs about 5 inches from the broiler. Broil about 5 minutes. Turn and broil about 5 minutes longer or until meat is done.

To grill on a charcoal grill, put kabobs about 5 inches above hot coals. Turn often until meat reaches desired doneness.

Dilled Potato Salad

MAKES 4 TO 6 SERVINGS

4 cups water

1½ teaspoons salt, divided

6 medium red potatoes (about 2 pounds)

¼ cup CRISCO® Oil

¼ cup tarragon vinegar

1 teaspoon sugar

1 clove garlic, minced

2 ribs celery, chopped

2 hard cooked eggs, chopped

⅓ cup chopped green onion

¾ cup mayonnaise

1½ teaspoons dried dill weed

Combine water and ½ teaspoon salt in 3-quart saucepan. Heat to boiling.

Shish Kabobs

Add potatoes. Cover. Simmer 30 to 40 minutes or until tender. Drain; cool slightly. Cut into ½-inch cubes. Place in medium serving bowl.

Blend CRISCO Oil, vinegar, sugar, garlic and remaining 1 teaspoon salt in small mixing bowl. Pour over potatoes. Cover and refrigerate about 2 hours.

Stir celery, hard cooked eggs and onion into potato mixture. Blend the mayonnaise and dill weed in small mixing bowl. Add to potato mixture. Mix well.

Cover and refrigerate at least 3 hours. Add additional salt and pepper, if desired.

Summer

Grilled Portobello Mushrooms and Summer Squash with Orange Vinaigrette

MAKES 4 SERVINGS

Orange Vinaigrette

- 2 cups freshly squeezed orange juice
- ¼ cup CRISCO® Oil
- 2 tablespoons rice wine vinegar
- 1 tablespoon cider vinegar
- 1 tablespoon fresh grated orange peel
- Salt and black pepper

Vegetables

- 4 whole portobello mushrooms, stems removed
- 4 thin yellow summer squash, cut lengthwise about ½-inch thick
- ¼ cup CRISCO Oil
- Salt and black pepper
- Salad greens
- 5 scallions, cut on the diagonal
- Toasted sesame seeds

To make the vinaigrette, in a saucepan over medium-high heat, bring the orange juice to a boil and reduce to about ½ cup. Remove from heat and whisk in the CRISCO Oil, rice wine vinegar, cider vinegar and orange peel. Add salt and pepper to taste. Chill until ready to use.

To grill the mushrooms and squash, brush them with CRISCO Oil and season with salt and pepper. Grill over medium-hot coals until vegetables are tender.

To serve, place salad greens on 4 plates. Arrange grilled vegetables on top of the greens and drizzle with the orange vinaigrette. Sprinkle with scallions and sesame seeds.

Summer

Father's Day Tie Cookie

MAKES 16 SERVINGS

- ⅔ **Butter Flavor CRISCO® Stick or ⅔ cup Butter Flavor CRISCO Shortening**
- ¾ **cup sugar**
- 1 **tablespoon plus 1 teaspoon milk**
- 1 **teaspoon vanilla**
- 1 **egg**
- 2 **cups all-purpose flour**
- 1½ **teaspoons baking powder**
- ¼ **teaspoon salt**

Combine CRISCO Shortening, sugar, milk and vanilla in large bowl. Beat at medium speed of electric mixer until well blended. Beat in egg. Combine flour, baking powder and salt. Mix into CRISCO mixture at low speed until well blended.

Preheat oven to 375°F. Line an 11×9-inch baking pan with parchment or waxed paper cut large enough to hang over the

long sides of the pan. Transfer dough to prepared pan and spread evenly in pan. Place a sheet of parchment or waxed paper over the dough to make spreading easier. Bake for 15 to 20 minutes or until set. Place on cooling rack and allow to cool completely.

Refrigerate before frosting; a chilled cookie is easier to frost. Lift cooled cookie out of pan using the parchment paper "handles."

Prepare Creamy Vanilla Frosting. Transfer frosting to a piping bag or a resealable plastic bag with the tip of the corner cut off. Outline shirt collar and tie on cookie with frosting. Decorate tie with Dad's favorite candies.

Creamy Vanilla Frosting

Combine ½ cup Butter Flavor CRISCO Shortening, 1 pound (4 cups) confectioners' sugar, ⅓ cup milk and 1 teaspoon vanilla in medium bowl. Beat at low speed of electric mixer until well blended. Scrape bowl. Beat at high speed for 2 minutes or until smooth and creamy.

Father's Day Brunch

WEEKEND POTATOES

•

BACON, AVOCADO AND CHEESE OMELET

•

FATHER'S DAY TIE COOKIE

Summer

To tint frosting for tie: Remove ½ cup of icing and add drops of food color for desired color.

An easy variation for kids: Use shoelace licorice for lines.

Give Dad a colored shirt: Reserve ½ cup frosting before tinting remaining frosting.

"Wrap" your present: Place pan cookie on a sheet of waxed paper and lower into a shirt box. Fold over parchment paper "handles" to protect cookie.

Summer

Weekend Potatoes

MAKES 6 SERVINGS

- 3 pounds russet potatoes
- 2 medium onions, halved lengthwise and thinly sliced crosswise
- 6 tablespoons Butter Flavor CRISCO® Stick or 6 tablespoons Butter Flavor CRISCO Shortening, divided
- 1 teaspoon salt
- 1 teaspoon black pepper
- 3 tablespoons finely chopped fresh chives

Place potatoes in a large stockpot; cover with water and boil for 20 minutes. Drain, cool slightly and chill in refrigerator overnight so potatoes won't fall apart when cutting.

Quarter potatoes lengthwise, then cut into ½-inch pieces.

In a 12-inch nonstick skillet, cook onions in 2 tablespoons CRISCO Shortening over moderately low heat, 10 to 15 minutes or until pale golden.

Push onions to the edges of the skillet. Add remaining 4 tablespoons CRISCO Shortening to the same skillet over moderately high heat. Add potatoes, salt and pepper; cook and stir 8 to 12 minutes or until golden. Gently mix onions back in with potatoes and toss in chives.

Bacon, Avocado and Cheese Omelet

MAKES 6 SERVINGS

- 2 cups finely chopped seeded tomato
- 2 jalapeño peppers*, or to taste, seeded and minced
- 4 tablespoons minced fresh cilantro
- 3 tablespoons fresh lime or lemon juice
  Salt and black pepper
- 12 eggs
- 6 tablespoons water
- 3 tablespoons Butter Flavor CRISCO® Stick or 3 tablespoons Butter Flavor CRISCO Shortening, divided
- 9 slices lean bacon, cooked and crumbled
- 2 small avocados, peeled and cut into ½-inch pieces
- 1½ cups coarsely grated Monterey Jack cheese

Bacon, Avocado and Cheese Omelet

Jalapeño peppers can sting and irritate the skin; wear rubber gloves when handling peppers and do not touch eyes. Wash hands after handling peppers.

To make the salsa, combine tomato, jalapeño, cilantro and lime juice in a small bowl. Season with salt and pepper; set aside.

Whisk together the eggs, water, salt and pepper in a medium bowl.

Heat ½ tablespoon CRISCO Shortening in an 8-inch skillet over medium-high heat. Pour ⅙ egg mixture into skillet. Cook for 1 minute or until almost set.

Sprinkle ½ the omelet with ⅙ the bacon, avocados and cheese. Cook the omelet for 1 minute or until set. Fold the omelet over the filling, transfer it to a plate and keep warm.

Repeat to make 6 omelets.

Serve topped with salsa.

Summer

Sweet Potato Salad

MAKES 6 SERVINGS

1½ pounds sweet potatoes or yams, scrubbed, quartered lengthwise, and cut crosswise into ¾-inch pieces

3 tablespoons cider vinegar

2 tablespoons sweet pickle relish

2 teaspoons Dijon mustard

½ teaspoon salt

¼ teaspoon freshly ground black pepper

½ cup CRISCO® Oil

2 green onions, trimmed and thinly sliced

¼ cup finely chopped red bell pepper

Place potatoes in vegetable steamer.* Place steamer over 2 inches of water in large pot. Cover pot. Bring to a boil on high heat. Steam potatoes 10 to 15 minutes or until tender when pierced with knife. Remove steamer from pan. Peel potatoes when cool enough to handle. Place potatoes in bowl.

While potatoes cool, combine vinegar, pickle relish, mustard, salt and pepper in jar with tight-fitting lid. Shake well. Add CRISCO Oil. Shake well again. Toss warm potatoes with dressing. Add green onions and red pepper. Serve at room temperature or chilled.

*Or, boil potatoes for 10 to 15 minutes.

Note: The salad can be made 1 day in advance, covered tightly with plastic wrap and refrigerated.

Labor Day Barbecue

SWEET POTATO SALAD

•

ASIAN GRILLED STEAKS WITH SPICY HERB SAUCE

•

RASPBERRY 'N' GINGER CREAM TART

Fall

Asian Grilled Steaks with Spicy Herb Sauce

MAKES 6 SERVINGS

⅔ cup CRISCO® Oil

3 tablespoons cooking sherry

3 tablespoons sugar

1½ tablespoons minced garlic

1 tablespoon sesame oil

1 teaspoon red pepper flakes

½ teaspoon salt

6 (1-inch-thick) strip steaks

Salt and black pepper, to taste

Spicy Herb Sauce

1 cup chopped cilantro, including stems

⅓ cup CRISCO Oil

3 tablespoons soy sauce

1 tablespoon fresh lime juice

1½ teaspoons minced garlic

½ teaspoon sesame oil

½ teaspoon minced jalapeño pepper*

Jalapeño peppers can sting and irritate the skin; wear rubber gloves when handling.

Stir together CRISCO Oil, sherry, sugar, garlic, sesame oil, pepper flakes and salt in a 9×13-inch baking dish. Stir until sugar is dissolved. Season steaks with salt and pepper. Add steaks, turning once to coat. Marinate for 1 hour, turning once.

To make Spicy Herb Sauce, stir together cilantro, CRISCO Oil, soy sauce, lime juice, garlic, sesame oil and jalapeño; set aside.

Preheat grill.

Remove steaks from marinade. Discard marinade. Cook steaks on a medium-hot grill for 3 to 4 minutes per side for medium-rare or until desired doneness. Top each steak with sauce.

Raspberry 'N' Ginger Cream Tart

MAKES 4 TO 6 SERVINGS

2 cups ground shortbread cookies

½ cup granulated sugar, divided

3 tablespoons very cold Butter Flavor CRISCO® Stick or 3 tablespoons very cold Butter Flavor CRISCO Shortening

2 tablespoons milk

Asian Grilled Steak with Spicy Herb Sauce

1½ teaspoons unflavored
    gelatin

⅓ cup very finely chopped
    crystallized ginger

1 teaspoon fresh lemon juice

⅛ teaspoon salt

2 cups heavy cream, divided

¾ cup sour cream

2 pints fresh raspberries

    Confectioners' sugar

Preheat oven to 350°F.

Blend shortbread cookies, ¼ cup sugar and CRISCO Shortening in food processor until mixture begins to clump together. Press onto bottom and up sides of a 10-inch removable bottom tart pan. Bake in the middle of the oven for about 15 minutes or until edges are lightly browned. Cool on rack.

Place 2 tablespoons milk in saucepan; sprinkle gelatin over milk and let stand 1 minute to soften. Add ginger, remaining ¼ cup sugar, lemon juice, salt and 1 cup heavy cream. Cook over moderate heat, stirring until gelatin and sugar are dissolved, about 6 to 7 minutes. Cool 1 hour. Whisk sour cream into the gelatin mixture until smooth.

Beat remaining 1 cup heavy cream in a bowl with electric mixer until soft peaks form. Gently fold gelatin mixture into heavy cream until well combined. Pour into crust and chill 8 hours or until set.

Top with fresh raspberries and a dusting of confectioners' sugar just before serving.

Fall

Sauerbraten

MAKES 6 TO 8 SERVINGS

- 3 large onions, sliced
- 8 tablespoons Butter Flavor CRISCO® Stick or 8 tablespoons Butter Flavor CRISCO Shortening, divided
- 3 cups cider vinegar
- 1 cup packed dark brown sugar
- 10 gingersnap cookies, crushed
- 20 whole cloves
- 10 peppercorns
- 6 bay leaves
- 3 cups (up to) water, divided
- 1 (4- to 6-pound) rump roast
- ½ cup sour cream
- ½ cup golden raisins

Cook the sliced onions in 2 tablespoons CRISCO Shortening until golden brown. Carefully add vinegar, brown sugar, cookies, cloves, peppercorns and bay leaves. Bring to a boil. Add 1 cup water; remove from heat and cool to room temperature.

Place rump roast in smallest possible container so marinade will cover. Pour marinade over meat adding more water to cover if needed. Cover with plastic wrap. Marinate in refrigerator for 3 days, turning meat 1 to 2 times per day. Remove roast from container; reserve marinade. Pat roast dry with paper towel.

Preheat oven to 350°F.

Melt 6 tablespoons CRISCO Shortening in a large skillet and brown roast on all sides. Place in roasting pan and roast, uncovered, for approximately 2½ hours or until internal temperature reaches 165°F. Let meat rest 20 minutes before carving.

Meanwhile, bring marinade to a boil and reduce by half; strain. Stir in sour cream and golden raisins. Serve sauce with roast.

Oktoberfest Menu

SAUERBRATEN

•

CREAMY HOT REUBEN DIP

•

CRISPY POTATO PANCAKES

Creamy Hot Reuben Dip

MAKES 6 TO 8 SERVINGS

- 4 tablespoons Butter Flavor CRISCO® Stick or 4 tablespoons Butter Flavor CRISCO Shortening
- 1 large onion, finely diced
- ½ pound corned beef, sliced and shredded
- 1 (8-ounce) package cream cheese, cubed
- 1½ cups sauerkraut, drained and chopped
- ½ cup ketchup
- ½ cup mayonnaise
- 2 tablespoons sweet pickle relish
- 2 tablespoons dill pickle relish
- 2 cups grated Swiss cheese

Melt CRISCO Shortening in a heavy 4-quart saucepan. Add onion and cook until golden brown. Add corned beef; cook over medium heat 3 minutes, stirring often. Drain fat.

Add cream cheese, 1 cube at a time, stirring after each addition. Add sauerkraut, ketchup, mayonnaise, pickle relish and cheese.

Stir until cheeses are melted and ingredients are well blended. Serve in a fondue pot or chafing dish with toasted mini rye triangles.

Crispy Potato Pancakes

MAKES 20 PANCAKES

- 4 cups freshly grated Idaho potato
- 4 eggs, beaten
- 1½ cups all-purpose flour
- 1 cup grated onion
- 2 teaspoons salt
- 2 teaspoons nutmeg CRISCO® Oil

Rinse potato under slowly running cold water about 5 minutes. Drain well; pat completely dry.

Mix eggs and flour together until smooth. Add onion, salt and nutmeg. Add to grated potatoes and mix well.

Heat ½-inch CRISCO Oil in a heavy skillet until almost smoking. Drop ½-cup portions potato batter into oil. Do not flatten. Turn after 2 minutes. Flatten slightly and cook an additional 2 minutes or until golden brown.

Drain on paper towels. Serve hot with applesauce, fried apples or a dollop of sour cream.

Pumpkin Seed
IDEAS

The month of October just isn't complete without carving a pumpkin. Make sure not to throw away the tasty seeds during the carving process. The whole family can partake in pumpkin seed baking. Try one of our delicious flavor twists or create your very own!

Preheat oven to 350°F. Separate the pumpkin seeds from the fibers. Wash, drain, and dry the seeds on paper towels. Coat 1½ cups seeds with 1 teaspoon CRISCO® Oil. Toss the seeds with salt (or omit salt and toss seeds with any of the suggested seasonings below), and spread them in a single layer on a baking sheet. Bake, stirring occasionally, 12 to 15 minutes or until golden brown.

Sugar & Spice Seeds
1 tablespoon sugar, ½ teaspoon ground cinnamon, and ⅛ teaspoon ground allspice

Deviled Seeds
1 tablespoon Worcestershire sauce and ¼ to ½ teaspoon chili powder

Italian Seeds
2 tablespoons grated Parmesan cheese and ½ teaspoon dried Italian seasoning

Spider Web Cupcakes

MAKES 24 CUPCAKES

Cupcakes

- 2 cups sifted cake flour
- 1⅓ cups granulated sugar
- 1 teaspoon salt
- 3 teaspoons baking powder
- ½ CRISCO® Stick or ½ cup CRISCO Shortening
- 1 cup milk, divided
- 2 eggs
- 1 teaspoon vanilla

Buttery Cream Frosting

- 4 cups confectioners' sugar
- ⅓ Butter Flavor CRISCO Stick or ⅓ cup Butter Flavor CRISCO Shortening
- 1½ teaspoons vanilla
- 7 to 8 tablespoons milk

  Red and yellow food coloring, mixed to make orange

  Black food coloring (or ½ cup melted chocolate chips)

Cupcakes

Preheat oven to 350°F.

Line cupcake pans with paper liners. Combine flour, sugar, salt and baking powder in mixing bowl. Add CRISCO Shortening and ⅔ cup milk.

Beat with electric mixer at medium speed for 2 minutes. Add eggs, remaining ⅓ cup milk and vanilla. Beat for 2 minutes. Pour into prepared cupcake pans.

Bake 15 to 20 minutes or until toothpick inserted in center comes out clean. Cool for 10 to 15 minutes on wire racks. Remove from pans. Cool completely on racks. Frost with Buttery Cream Frosting.

Buttery Cream Frosting

Combine confectioners' sugar, CRISCO Shortening and vanilla in medium mixing bowl. Slowly blend in milk to desired consistency. Beat on high speed for 5 minutes or until smooth and creamy.

Reserve ½ cup frosting to tint orange or black.* Frost each cupcake with remaining frosting. Using a piping bag or a plastic zip-top bag with the corner cut off, pipe a spider web onto each cupcake using colored frosting. Decorate as desired.

*1 or 2 drops of food color can be used to tint each ½ cup of frosting.

Caramel Apples

MAKES 12 APPLES

- 2 cups heavy cream
- 2 cups sugar
- ¼ Butter Flavor CRISCO® Stick or ¼ cup Butter Flavor CRISCO Shortening
- ½ cup dark corn syrup
- 12 medium McIntosh apples, washed and stemmed
- 12 wooden craft sticks

Line baking sheet with parchment paper; set aside. Fill about half of a large bowl with ice water.

Place cream, sugar, CRISCO Shortening and corn syrup in a heavy-bottomed saucepan; bring to a boil over medium heat. Continue cooking until the temperature registers 245°F on a candy thermometer, 10 to 12 minutes. Remove from heat and briefly plunge the saucepan into ice water to stop the caramel from cooking. Remove from ice water and let mixture cool for a few minutes.

Insert a craft stick into the stem end of each apple. Dip 1 apple into the caramel; coat the top and sides with caramel using a spoon. Transfer to prepared baking sheet to cool. Repeat with remaining apples.

Optional Toppings: Chocolate covered toffee bits, crushed Macadamia nuts, crushed peanuts, seasonal sprinkles, tinted coconut or chopped candy corn.

Note: Use 5-inch craft sticks, ¼-inch in diameter. Garnish as desired, or serve in seasonal cupcake liners.

Harvest Moon Cake

MAKES 1 (8-INCH) SQUARE CAKE

Cake

- 1 cup granulated sugar
- ½ CRISCO® Stick or ½ cup CRISCO Shortening
- 2 eggs
- 1 cup fresh pumpkin purée or canned solid-pack pumpkin*
- ¼ teaspoon salt
- 1¾ cups cake flour
- 1 teaspoon baking powder

- ½ **teaspoon baking soda**
- ¼ **teaspoon ground cinnamon**
- ¼ **teaspoon ground ginger**
- ¼ **teaspoon ground nutmeg**
- 1 **cup miniature semisweet chocolate chips**

Add 2 tablespoons water to pumpkin if using canned pumpkin.

Frosting
- ⅓ **cup maple syrup**
- ¼ **CRISCO® Stick or ¼ cup CRISCO Shortening**
- ¼ **cup unsalted butter, softened**
- ¼ **teaspoon salt**
- 2 **cups confectioners' sugar**

Garnish (optional)
Additional miniature semi-sweet chocolate chips

Preheat oven to 350°F.

Spray 8-inch square cake pan with CRISCO No-Stick Cooking Spray.

Combine granulated sugar, ½ cup CRISCO Shortening and eggs in large bowl. Beat with electric mixer at medium speed until creamy. Beat in pumpkin and salt until blended. Combine flour, baking powder, baking soda, cinnamon, ginger and

Harvest Moon Cake

nutmeg in small bowl. Add to pumpkin mixture gradually, beating at low speed after each addition just until mixed. Stir in chocolate chips with a wooden spoon. Pour into prepared pan.

Bake 40 to 45 minutes or until toothpick inserted in center comes out clean. Cool 10 minutes before removing from pan. Invert cake on wire rack. Cool completely. Place cake on serving plate.

For frosting, combine maple syrup, CRISCO Shortening, butter and salt in medium bowl. Beat with electric mixer until blended. Mix in confectioners' sugar gradually, beating until creamy. Frost top and sides of cake. Garnish with additional chocolate chips.

Brownstone Pumpkin Pie

MAKES 6 TO 8 SERVINGS

1 Classic CRISCO® Single Pie Crust (Recipe on page 16)
⅔ cup packed brown sugar
½ cup granulated sugar
2 tablespoons all-purpose flour
1 teaspoon ground cinnamon
½ teaspoon salt
½ teaspoon ground allspice
½ teaspoon ground cloves
½ teaspoon ground ginger
1½ cups canned solid-pack pumpkin
2 tablespoons molasses
3 large eggs
1 cup whipping cream

Preheat oven to 375°F.

On a lightly floured surface, roll the pie dough out into a circle slightly larger than the pie pan. Roll the pastry around the rolling pin and unroll the pastry into the pan. With the knuckles of your fingers, gently ease the pastry into the pan. Cut off excess pastry over the edges of the pan and flute edge of pie crust.

Whisk brown sugar and next 7 ingredients together in large bowl. Whisk in pumpkin, molasses and eggs. Add cream; stir well. Pour mixture into crust.

Bake 35 to 45 minutes or until the filling is set in the center. Let cool on a rack.

Turkey with Herb Dressing

MAKES 10 TO 14 SERVINGS

16 cups diced (½-inch thick) bread cubes
⅓ cup dried parsley flakes
2 teaspoons salt
2 teaspoons crushed rosemary
2 teaspoons ground thyme
1 teaspoon ground sage

½ CRISCO® Stick or ½ cup CRISCO Shortening
1 cup coarsely chopped onion
1 cup coarsely chopped celery
1½ cups chicken broth
1 turkey (14 to 15 pounds)
   Butter Flavor CRISCO Shortening for basting

Turkey with Herb Dressing

Preheat oven to 325°F.

Combine bread cubes, parsley, salt, rosemary, thyme and sage in a large bowl. Toss to mix.

Melt CRISCO Shortening in a skillet over medium heat. Mix in onion and celery; cook for 3 minutes, stirring occasionally. Toss with the bread mixture. Add chicken broth, mixing gently until ingredients are thoroughly blended.

Rinse turkey with cold water; pat dry, inside and out, with paper towels. Fill body and neck cavities with the stuffing. Fasten neck skin to back with a skewer. Bring wing tips onto back of bird. Push drumsticks under band of skin at tail, if present, or tie to tail with cord.

Place turkey breast-side-up on a rack in a shallow roasting pan. Insert ovenproof meat thermometer in the thickest part of the inner thigh muscle; tip should not touch bone.

Roast for 4 to 5 hours or until thermometer registers 180°F to 185°F; baste frequently with CRISCO Shortening during roasting.

Remove stuffing immediately from bird. For easier carving, let stand 15 to 20 minutes after removing from oven.

Fall

Herbed Green Bean Casserole

MAKES 8 SERVINGS

- **1 cup freshly grated Parmesan cheese**
- **¾ cup dried breadcrumbs, divided**
- **2 teaspoons dried basil**
- **2 teaspoons parsley**
- **1 teaspoon garlic powder**
- **1 teaspoon dried oregano**
- **½ teaspoon salt**
- **½ teaspoon dried thyme**
- **½ teaspoon black pepper**
- **½ cup CRISCO® Oil**
- **2 (14-ounce) cans green beans, drained**

Preheat oven to 350°F.

Combine first 9 ingredients in a large bowl. Toss well. Add CRISCO Oil to breadcrumb mixture; stir well. Reserve 2 tablespoons breadcrumb mixture for top of casserole. Combine green beans and breadcrumb mixture in an ovenproof dish and sprinkle with the reserved crumb mixture.

Bake for about 30 minutes or until the top is golden and crispy.

Note: You can replace the canned beans with frozen or blanched and cooled fresh beans. The dried breadcrumbs and herbs can be replaced with Italian-style breadcrumbs.

Thanksgiving Menu

TURKEY WITH HERB DRESSING

•

HERBED GREEN BEAN CASSEROLE

•

CRANBERRY ORANGE SAUCED SWEET POTATOES

•

INDIAN SUMMER PUMPKIN BREAD

•

BROWNSTONE PUMPKIN PIE

Cranberry Orange Sauced Sweet Potatoes

MAKES 6 SERVINGS

- **6 medium sweet potatoes or yams**
- **¼ CRISCO® Stick or ¼ cup CRISCO Shortening**
- **¼ cup packed light brown sugar**
- **¼ cup fresh orange juice**
- **¼ cup water**
- **½ teaspoon salt**
- **1¼ cups fresh cranberries, rinsed**
- **½ teaspoon cornstarch**
- **2 tablespoons cold water**

Preheat oven to 400°F.

Wash sweet potatoes and pat dry. Prick with a fork, place in a shallow baking dish and bake for 40 to 50 minutes or until soft.

During the last 10 minutes of baking, prepare sauce. Melt CRISCO Shortening in a medium saucepan. Add brown sugar, orange juice, ¼ cup water and salt, stirring over low heat until sugar dissolves. Add cranberries and bring to a boil. Reduce heat and simmer covered for 5 minutes or until cranberries start to pop. Mix cornstarch with 2 tablespoons cold water in a small bowl, blending until smooth. Stir into cranberries; cook, stirring constantly, until sauce comes to a boil. Reduce heat and cook 1 to 2 minutes or until mixture is slightly thickened.

Make a lengthwise cut in the center of each potato; press open from bottom. Place sweet potatoes on a serving platter. Top each with cranberry sauce.

Yam Vines

Save the tops of your Thanksgiving yams and watch them grow!

What you'll need: Yam (or sweet potato), knife, vegetable brush, toothpicks, jar, and water.

Cut off the bottom third of the yam. Scrub the top well with warm water and a brush. Then stick 4 toothpicks into the center of the yam top so that it will sit in a jar full of water. Place the jar in bright light, but not direct sun. Check your yam every day to make sure the water always covers the cut part. After about a week, you will see stringy white roots growing out of the cut part. Soon purplish leaves will sprout from the top. The yam vine will grow fast, and soon the leaves will be bright green.

Indian Summer Pumpkin Bread

MAKES 2 LOAVES OR 36 MUFFINS

3½ cups all-purpose flour

2 teaspoons baking soda

1 teaspoon baking powder

1 teaspoon ground cloves

1 teaspoon ground cinnamon

1 teaspoon ground nutmeg

½ teaspoon salt

3 cups granulated sugar

2 cups solid-pack pumpkin

1 cup CRISCO® Oil

3 eggs

1 cup chopped walnuts

1 cup raisins

1½ cups confectioners' sugar

1 teaspoon grated
   orange peel

6 teaspoons orange juice

   Additional chopped walnuts

Preheat oven to 350°F.

Spray 2 loaf pans with CRISCO No-Stick Cooking Spray or line muffin pans with paper liners.

Combine flour, baking soda, baking powder, cloves, cinnamon, nutmeg and salt in a medium bowl. Set aside. In the bowl of an electric mixer, combine the sugar, pumpkin, CRISCO Oil and eggs. Mix until well blended. Add dry ingredients and mix well. Stir in the walnuts and raisins with wooden spoon.

Divide batter between prepared loaf pans or muffin pans. Bake for 50 to 55 minutes for bread or 20 to 25 minutes for muffins. Cool in pans on a wire rack for 15 minutes. Remove from pans and cool completely.

To make glaze, combine confectioners' sugar, orange peel and orange juice in small bowl. Stir with spoon to blend. Spoon over top of cooled loaves or muffins. Sprinkle with additional walnuts.

Peppermint Cookies

MAKES ABOUT 3 DOZEN COOKIES

1 cup packed light
   brown sugar

¾ Butter Flavor CRISCO®
   Stick or ¾ cup Butter
   Flavor CRISCO
   Shortening

2 tablespoons milk

1 tablespoon vanilla

1 egg

1¾ cups all-purpose flour

1 teaspoon salt

¾ teaspoon baking soda

⅔ cup crushed peppermint
   candy canes or
   peppermint candies*
   plus extra for garnish,
   if desired

*To crush candy canes,
place them in a resealable
plastic bag. Run a rolling
pin over the bag of candy
to break the candy canes
into very small pieces.*

Preheat oven to 375°F.

Combine brown sugar,
CRISCO Shortening, milk
and vanilla in large bowl.
Beat at medium speed
with electric mixer until
well blended.

Beat egg into CRISCO
mixture. Combine flour,
salt and baking soda. Mix
into CRISCO mixture at low
speed just until blended.
Stir in crushed candy.

Shape dough into 1-inch
balls. Place 2 inches apart
on ungreased baking
sheets. Bake 1 baking
sheet at a time for 8 to
10 minutes for chewy
cookies or 11 to 13 minutes
for crisp cookies. DO NOT
OVERBAKE. Cool 2 minutes
on baking sheet. Remove
cookies to rack to cool
completely.

Winter

Raspberry Linzer Rounds

MAKES 2 DOZEN COOKIES

1¼ cups granulated sugar

1 Butter Flavor CRISCO® Stick
or 1 cup Butter Flavor
CRISCO Shortening

2 eggs

¼ cup light corn syrup or
regular pancake syrup

1 teaspoon vanilla

1 teaspoon almond extract

2 cups plus 4 tablespoons
all-purpose flour, divided

1 cup ground almonds

¾ teaspoon baking powder

½ teaspoon baking soda

½ teaspoon salt

½ cup SMUCKER'S® Raspberry
Preserves (seedless)

Confectioners' sugar
(optional)

Combine sugar and CRISCO Shortening in large bowl. Beat at medium speed with electric mixer until well blended. Add eggs, syrup, vanilla and almond extract. Beat until well blended and fluffy.

Combine 2 cups flour, almonds, baking powder, baking soda and salt. Add gradually to CRISCO mixture at low speed. Mix until well blended. Divide dough into 4 quarters. Wrap each quarter of dough with plastic wrap. Refrigerate several hours or overnight.

Preheat oven to 375°F. Place sheets of foil on countertop for cooling cookies.

Spread 1 tablespoon or more flour on large sheet of waxed paper. Place ¼ dough on floured paper. Flatten slightly with hands. Turn dough over and cover with another large sheet of waxed paper. Roll dough to ¼-inch thickness. Remove top sheet of waxed paper.

Cut out with 2- to 2½-inch floured crinkled round cutters. Transfer to ungreased baking sheet with large spatula; place 2 inches apart. Repeat with remaining dough. Cut out centers of half of cookies with ½- to ¾-inch round cutter.

Bake 1 baking sheet at a time for 5 to 9 minutes, depending on the size of cookies (bake smaller, thinner cookies about 5 minutes; larger cookies, about 9 minutes). DO NOT OVERBAKE. Cool 2 minutes on

baking sheet. Remove cookies to foil to cool completely.

Spread a small amount of SMUCKER'S® Raspberry Preserves on uncut cookies.

Top with cut-out cookies, bottom sides down, to make sandwiches. Sift confectioners' sugar over cookies, if desired.

Winter

Pralines

MAKES 3 DOZEN

1½ cups packed brown sugar

1 cup granulated sugar

1 can (5⅓ ounces)
   evaporated milk

1 tablespoon light corn syrup

3 tablespoons Butter Flavor
   CRISCO® Stick or
   3 tablespoons Butter
   Flavor CRISCO Shortening

½ teaspoon vanilla

1½ cups coarsely chopped
   pecans

¼ teaspoon cream of tartar

Lightly grease baking sheet
with CRISCO Shortening;
set aside.

In 3-quart saucepan combine
brown sugar, granulated
sugar, evaporated milk and
corn syrup. Heat to boiling
over medium heat, stirring
constantly. Cover and boil
for 1 minute. Uncover. Insert
candy thermometer. Cook over
medium heat, without stirring,
to 235°F. Remove from heat.

Add CRISCO Shortening,
vanilla, pecans and cream of
tartar. Stir with wooden spoon
until mixture thickens slightly.
Do not overstir. Quickly drop by
rounded tablespoonfuls onto
prepared baking sheet. Cool
until firm.

Cherry Chocolate Chippies

MAKES ABOUT 4 DOZEN COOKIES

1¼ cups packed light
   brown sugar

¾ Butter Flavor CRISCO® Stick
   or ¾ cup Butter Flavor
   CRISCO Shortening

1 teaspoon vanilla

1 teaspoon almond extract

1 egg

1¾ cups all-purpose flour

1 teaspoon salt

¾ teaspoon baking soda

1 cup (6 ounces) semisweet
   chocolate chips

1 cup well-drained
   maraschino cherries,
   coarsely chopped

Cherry Chocolate Chippies

Preheat oven to 375°F.

Place sheets of foil on counter-top for cooling cookies. Place sugar, CRISCO Shortening, vanilla and almond extract in large bowl. Beat at medium speed of electric mixer until well blended. Add egg; beat well.

Combine flour, salt and baking soda. Add to CRISCO mixture; beat at low speed just until blended. Stir in chocolate chips and cherries with a spoon.

Drop dough by rounded tablespoonfuls, 2 inches apart, onto ungreased baking sheets. Bake 1 baking sheet at a time for 8 to 10 minutes for chewy cookies, or 11 to 13 minutes for crisp cookies. DO NOT OVERBAKE. Cool 2 minutes on baking sheet. Remove cookies to foil to cool completely.

Winter

Classic Sugar Cookies

MAKES ABOUT 5 DOZEN COOKIES

- 1 **Butter Flavor CRISCO® Stick or 1 cup Butter Flavor CRISCO Shortening**
- 1½ **cups granulated sugar**
- ½ **cup packed brown sugar**
- 2 **tablespoons milk**
- 3 **eggs**
- 1 **teaspoon vanilla**
- 4 to 5 **cups all-purpose flour**
- 1½ **teaspoons baking soda**
- 1½ **teaspoons cream of tartar**
- 1 **teaspoon salt**
  Buttery Cream Frosting (recipe page 78)

Combine CRISCO Shortening and sugars. Beat on medium speed of electric mixture until well combined. Add milk. Beat in eggs 1 at a time; add vanilla and mix well. Combine flour, baking soda, cream of tartar and salt. Mix into CRISCO mixture until well blended. Chill for 1 hour.

Preheat oven to 350°F.

Roll out ⅓ dough at a time, to about ¼-inch thickness on a floured surface.

Cut out with cookie cutters. Place 2 inches apart on ungreased baking sheet. Sprinkle with colored sugars and decors or leave plain to frost when cooled.

Bake for 5 to 6 minutes or until edges are slightly golden. Remove immediately to cooling rack.

"Exploding" Party Favors

Play tug of war with these party favors, and watch them explode with candy!

What you'll need: Gold and silver wrapping paper, tape, scissors, ruler, small wrapped candies, and colored ribbons.

These party favors were popular in France before the mid-1800s! The size of the snapper you want to make will determine how big your paper should be and how much candy you'll need. For starters, you might want to use a sheet of wrapping paper that's 6×10 inches. Overlap the paper ½ inch on the long sides to form a tube and tape the edges together. Put 12 to 15 candies in the middle of the tube. Twist the ends of the paper, about 3 inches from the end. Tie each twist with a piece of ribbon, making a bow with streamers. Open each end of the paper so that it flares outward, and push the ends together so the center puffs up. To make your snapper explode candy, hold one end while a friend holds the other. Tug and shake the snapper until the paper breaks.

Miniature Monte Cristos

MAKES 2 DOZEN

6 slices soft white bread, crusts trimmed

Mustard

6 very thin slices fully cooked ham

6 very thin slices fully cooked turkey

6 very thin slices Swiss cheese

1 cup buttermilk baking mix

2 eggs

1 can (5⅓ ounces) evaporated milk

¼ teaspoon salt

⅛ teaspoon ground cinnamon CRISCO® Oil for frying

Flatten each slice of trimmed bread with rolling pin. Spread slices with mustard. Top each with 1 slice each ham, turkey and Swiss cheese. Roll bread tightly, using plastic wrap to assist in rolling. Wrap very tightly in plastic wrap to assure an even log shape. Chill for 30 minutes.

For batter, in medium bowl beat together baking mix and eggs. Add evaporated milk, salt and cinnamon.

In deep-fat fryer or deep saucepan heat 1½ inches CRISCO Oil to 375°F. Unwrap each roll and secure with 4 wooden picks. With serrated knife, slice each roll into 4 pieces (each secured with wooden pick).

Dip each piece in batter, allowing some batter to be absorbed. Fry a few at a time in hot oil for 1 to 2 minutes, or until deep golden brown, turning frequently. Drain on paper towels. Serve immediately or keep warm in 175°F oven. Serve with spicy mustard sauce, if desired.

Tip: To make a day ahead, prepare and fry as directed. Cool. Cover and refrigerate. Reheat in single layer on baking sheet in 425°F oven for 8 to 10 minutes.

Winter

Swiss Cheese, Spinach and Bacon Appetizer Tarts

MAKES 2¹/₂ DOZEN

1 Classic CRISCO® Double Pie Crust (page 16)

Filling:

- **2 eggs, slightly beaten**
- **½ cup sour cream**
- **¾ teaspoon mustard**
- **¼ teaspoon salt**
- **⅛ teaspoon ground nutmeg**
- **¼ teaspoon ground red pepper**
- **¾ cup shredded Swiss cheese**
- **3 tablespoons finely chopped onion**
- **2 tablespoons frozen chopped spinach, squeezed dry**
- **2 tablespoons crisp cooked bacon, finely chopped**
- **Ground nutmeg (optional)**

Preheat oven to 400°F.

Make Classic CRISCO Double Pie Crust per recipe directions.

Roll dough to ⅛-inch thickness on a lightly floured surface. Cut with a floured 2¾-inch round cutter. Fit carefully into 1¾-inch muffin cups so dough is not stretched. Press edges against rims.

For filling, blend eggs, sour cream, mustard, salt, nutmeg and red pepper. Stir in cheese, onion, spinach and bacon. Spoon a scant 1 tablespoon filling into each tart shell. Sprinkle with nutmeg, if desired.

Bake for 15 to 20 minutes or until filling is golden brown.

Cream Puff Appetizers

MAKES 2 DOZEN

- **½ cup water**
- **¼ Butter Flavor CRISCO® Stick or ¼ cup Butter Flavor CRISCO Shortening**
- **½ cup all-purpose flour**
- **⅛ teaspoon salt**

- **2 eggs**
- **1 package (3 ounces) cream cheese, softened**
- **⅓ cup sour cream**
- **4 teaspoons cocktail sauce**
- **¼ teaspoon dried tarragon leaves**

Swiss Cheese, Spinach and Bacon Appetizer Tarts

⅛ teaspoon black pepper

Dash garlic powder

2 cans (6¼ ounces each) tiny shrimp, rinsed, drained and chopped

1 can (8 ounces) water chestnuts, drained and finely chopped

2 tablespoons finely chopped green onions

Salt to taste

Preheat oven to 400°F.

In medium saucepan combine water and CRISCO Shortening. Heat to rolling boil. Add flour and salt, stirring until mixture forms a ball. Continue to cook and stir for 1 minute. Remove from heat. Add eggs all at once, beating until smooth.

Drop by teaspoonfuls at least 1½ inches apart onto ungreased baking sheet. Bake for 20 to 30 minutes or until golden brown. Cool away from draft. Meanwhile, prepare filling.

In medium mixing bowl blend cream cheese and sour cream. Stir in cocktail sauce, tarragon, pepper and garlic powder. Add shrimp, water chestnuts and green onions. Mix thoroughly. Cover and refrigerate for at least 30 minutes. Season to taste with salt.

To fill, cut off tops of cooled cream puffs. Remove dough filaments from inside. Fill with shrimp mixture and replace tops.

Winter

Fried Chicken Wings with Sweet-Sour Sauce

MAKES 4 SERVINGS

- 2 pounds chicken wings
- 2 tablespoons dry mustard
- 1 tablespoon water
- 1 cup all-purpose flour
- 1 teaspoon salt
- ½ teaspoon black pepper
- 1 cup CRISCO® Oil
- 1 cup SMUCKER'S® Apricot Preserves
- ¼ cup cider vinegar
- 2 tablespoons brown sugar
- 1 teaspoon dry mustard
- ½ teaspoon ground ginger

Slice off and discard wing tips. Rinse and pat wings dry. Mix dry mustard and water; pour over wings and toss. Combine flour, salt and pepper in a large resealable plastic bag; add chicken and toss to coat.

Heat CRISCO Oil in a large skillet over medium-high heat. Fry wings until golden brown, about 25 minutes. Drain on paper towels.

Combine remaining ingredients in a medium saucepan over medium heat. Bring to a boil and cook until sauce reduces by a third. Toss sauce and chicken wings.

Sweet Potato Crisps

MAKES 4 TO 6 SERVINGS

- 3 medium sweet potatoes
- 3 tablespoons CRISCO® Oil
- ¼ cup sugar
- ½ to 1 teaspoon cinnamon
- ½ teaspoon salt

Preheat oven to 450°F.

Peel potatoes and cut into ¾-inch thick slices. Pour CRISCO Oil into 13×9-inch baking pan.

Heat for 3 minutes. Remove pan from oven.

Arrange sweet potato slices in single layer in pan. Return pan to oven. Bake 10 minutes. Turn potatoes with spatula. Sprinkle potatoes with sugar, cinnamon and salt. Bake 10 to 15 minutes or until potatoes are browned. Drain on paper towels.

Fried Chicken Wings ▶
with Sweet-Sour Sauce

Oven–Barbecued Ribs

MAKES 4 SERVINGS

- ¼ cup CRISCO® Oil
- 3 to 4 pounds pork spareribs, cut into serving-size pieces
- ½ cup finely diced onion
- ⅓ cup finely diced celery
- ¼ cup finely grated carrot
- ⅓ cup ketchup
- ¼ cup packed brown sugar
- 1 tablespoon prepared mustard
- 1½ teaspoons chili powder
- ½ teaspoon salt
- ¼ teaspoon cayenne

Preheat oven to 350°F.

Heat CRISCO Oil in large skillet.

Add ribs. Brown over medium-high heat. Remove ribs from skillet; set aside. Discard drippings, reserving 2 tablespoons in skillet. Arrange ribs in 13×9-inch baking dish. Cover dish with aluminum foil. Bake 1 hour.

Meanwhile, heat 2 tablespoons reserved drippings in skillet. Add onion, celery and carrot. Cook and stir over moderate heat until tender. Stir in remaining ingredients. Simmer, stirring occasionally, about 5 minutes.

Drain ribs. Baste generously with sauce. Cover with foil. Bake 30 to 60 minutes or until tender.

Texas Chili

MAKES 6 TO 8 SERVINGS

- ¼ cup all-purpose flour
- 1½ pounds beef stew meat, cut into ¾-inch cubes
- 5 tablespoons CRISCO® Oil, divided
- 1 medium onion, chopped
- 2 cloves garlic, minced
- 2 cans (16 ounces each) whole tomatoes, undrained and chopped
- 2 cans (16 ounces each) kidney beans, drained
- 1 can (8 ounces) tomato sauce
- 2 tablespoons chili powder
- 1 teaspoon crushed red pepper
- 1 teaspoon salt
- 1 teaspoon ground cumin
- ¼ teaspoon cayenne pepper
- ¼ teaspoon ground oregano

Oven-Barbecued Ribs

Place flour in large resealable plastic bag. Add beef and shake to coat. Heat 3 tablespoons CRISCO Oil in large saucepan. Add beef and any remaining flour. Brown over medium-high heat. Remove beef from saucepan; set aside.

Heat remaining 2 tablespoons CRISCO Oil in the same saucepan. Add onion and garlic. Cook and stir over moderate heat until onion is tender. Stir in beef and remaining ingredients. Heat to boiling. Cover. Reduce heat. Simmer, stirring occasionally, about 1 hour. Uncover. Simmer, stirring occasionally, 30 to 60 minutes more or until beef is tender.

Winter

Chocolate Fondue

MAKES 1¹/₂ CUPS

- ⅓ cup heavy cream
- 1½ teaspoons grated orange peel
- 3 tablespoons Butter Flavor CRISCO® Stick or 3 tablespoons Butter Flavor CRISCO Shortening
- 8 ounces semisweet chocolate chips
- 3 teaspoons orange extract, divided
- Pound cake or angel food cake, cut into chunks
- Strawberries
- Kiwis, peeled and sliced
- Pears, sliced
- Bananas, sliced
- Peeled orange segments

Bring heavy cream and orange peel to simmer in heavy saucepan. Reduce heat to low. Add CRISCO Shortening, chocolate chips and 1½ teaspoons orange extract; whisk until mixture is smooth. Remove fondue from heat and blend in remaining 1½ teaspoons orange extract.

Transfer to fondue pot. Place over candle or canned heat burner. Make sure heat is low. Serve with cake pieces and fruit for dipping.

Profiteroles

MAKES 2 DOZEN

½ **cup water**

¼ **Butter Flavor CRISCO® Stick
    or ¼ cup Butter Flavor
    CRISCO Shortening**

½ **cup all-purpose flour**

⅛ **teaspoon salt**

2 **eggs**

**Ice cream (your favorite
    flavor)**

**SMUCKER'S® Chocolate
    Sundae Syrup**

Preheat oven to 400°F.

In medium saucepan, combine water and CRISCO Shortening. Heat to a rolling boil. Add flour and salt, stirring until mixture forms a ball. Continue to cook and stir for 1 minute. Remove from heat. Add eggs all at once, beating until smooth.

Drop by teaspoonfuls at least 1½ inches apart onto ungreased baking sheet. Bake for 20 to 30 minutes or until golden brown. Cool away from draft.

To fill, cut off tops of cooled cream puffs. Remove dough filaments from inside. Fill with a small scoop of your favorite ice cream. Replace tops and drizzle chocolate syrup on top.

Winter

Peanut Butter Kisses

MAKES 6 TO 7½ DOZEN COOKIES

1 Butter Flavor CRISCO® Stick
   or 1 cup Butter Flavor
   CRISCO Shortening

1 cup Jif® Creamy
   Peanut Butter

1 cup packed brown sugar

1 cup granulated sugar

2 eggs

¼ cup milk

2 teaspoons vanilla

3¼ cups all-purpose flour

2 teaspoons baking soda

1 teaspoon salt

   Granulated sugar for rolling

72 to 90 milk chocolate kisses
   or stars, unwrapped

Preheat oven to 375°F.

Combine CRISCO Shortening, Jif® Peanut Butter, brown sugar and granulated sugar in large bowl. Beat at medium speed of electric mixer until well blended. Beat in eggs, milk and vanilla. Combine flour, baking soda and salt. Mix into peanut butter mixture at low speed until just blended. Dough will be stiff.

Form dough into 1-inch balls. Roll in granulated sugar. Place 2 inches apart on ungreased baking sheet.

Bake for 8 minutes. Press milk chocolate kiss into center of each cookie. Return to oven. Bake 3 minutes. Cool 2 minutes on baking sheet. Remove to cooling rack.

Variation:

Jam-Filled Peanut Butter Kisses: Prepare recipe as directed. Bake at 375°F for 8 minutes. Press handle of wooden spoon gently in center of each cookie. Return to oven. Bake 3 minutes. Finish as directed. Fill cooled cookies with favorite SMUCKER'S® jam.

Winter

Shrimp Jambalaya

MAKES 6 TO 8 SERVINGS

- 3 tablespoons CRISCO® Stick or 3 tablespoons CRISCO Shortening
- ¼ pound diced cooked ham
- ¾ cup chopped green bell pepper, divided
- ½ cup chopped onion
- ½ cup chopped celery
- ⅓ cup chopped green onion
- 1 garlic clove, minced
- 2 cups chicken broth
- 1 can (14½ ounce) tomatoes, diced
- ¼ cup minced fresh parsley
- ½ teaspoon salt
- ¼ teaspoon dried leaf thyme
- ⅛ teaspoon black pepper

- ⅛ teaspoon chili powder or ground red pepper
- 1 bay leaf
- 1 cup uncooked rice
- ¾ pound medium cooked shrimp, peeled and deveined

Melt CRISCO Shortening in a large heavy skillet over medium heat. Stir in ham, ½ cup bell pepper, onion, celery, green onion and garlic. Cook for 5 minutes or until onion is tender, stirring occasionally.

Stir in chicken broth, tomatoes, parsley, salt, thyme, pepper, chili powder and bay leaf; cover and bring to a boil. Add rice gradually, stirring with a fork.

Cover and simmer for 20 minutes or until rice is tender. Mix in shrimp and remaining ¼ cup green pepper. Simmer uncovered for 5 minutes longer. Remove bay leaf before serving.

Mardi Gras Menu

SHRIMP JAMBALAYA

•

QUICK AND EASY BEANS AND RICE

•

BOURBON STREET BEIGNET PUFFS

Winter

Bourbon Street Beignet Puffs

MAKES 2¹/₂ DOZEN

CRISCO® Shortening for deep frying

1 **cup water**

½ **cup butter**

¼ **teaspoon salt**

1 **cup all-purpose flour**

1 **tablespoon plus 1½ teaspoons granulated sugar**

4 **eggs (at room temperature)**

1½ **teaspoons vanilla**

Confectioners' sugar

Heat 2 or 3 inches CRISCO Shortening to 365°F in deep fryer or deep saucepan.

In a separate saucepan, combine water, butter and salt. Bring to a boil.

Add flour and sugar. Reduce heat to medium and stir until dough is smooth, glossy and comes away from side of pan. Remove from heat. Stir 2 minutes to cool slightly. Add eggs 1 at a time. Beat after each addition until well blended. Beat in vanilla.

Drop by teaspoonfuls, a few at a time, into hot CRISCO Shortening. Fry several minutes or until deep golden brown. Turn as needed for even browning. Remove with slotted metal spoon. Drain on paper towels. Roll in confectioners' sugar. Serve warm.

Quick and Easy Red Beans and Rice

MAKES 6 SERVINGS

2 tablespoons CRISCO® Oil

1 cup chopped onion

½ cup chopped green bell pepper

¼ cup chopped celery

3 to 4 cloves garlic, minced

½ pound ham, cut into ½-inch cubes

¼ pound smoked sausage, sliced thin

1 bay leaf

½ teaspoon dried thyme

1 cup chicken or beef stock, or water

2 (15-ounce) cans red kidney beans, rinsed and drained

½ teaspoon salt

¼ teaspoon black pepper

⅛ teaspoon cayenne, more or less to taste
Cooked rice

Chopped onions

Hot sauce

Heat the CRISCO Oil in a large heavy pot over medium heat. Add the onion, bell pepper, celery and garlic. Cook about 5 minutes, stirring often, until the vegetables are soft. Add the ham, sausage, bay leaf and thyme. Cook for 3 to 5 minutes, stirring often.

Add the stock or water, beans, salt, pepper and cayenne. Bring to a simmer and cook about 20 minutes, stirring occasionally.

Serve over cooked rice with chopped onions and your favorite hot sauce on the side.

Winter

Corned Beef Dinner

MAKES 12 SERVINGS

- 1 corned beef brisket (about 5 pounds)
- 2 medium onions, peeled and quartered
- 4 peppercorns
- 1 bay leaf
- ½ teaspoon rosemary, crushed
- 1 quart water
- 6 medium potatoes (about 2 pounds), peeled and quartered
- 6 medium carrots, peeled and cut into 2-inch pieces
- 1 cup celery, cut into 2-inch pieces
- 1 medium head green cabbage, cut into wedges

Horseradish Sauce

- 2 tablespoons CRISCO® Stick or 2 tablespoons CRISCO Shortening
- 2 tablespoons all-purpose flour
- ½ teaspoon salt
- ⅛ teaspoon black pepper
- 1 egg yolk
- 1 cup milk
- 1 tablespoon lemon juice
- 2 teaspoons prepared horseradish, or to taste

Put beef into a large Dutch oven with a tight-fitting cover. Add onions, peppercorns, bay leaf, rosemary and water. Bring to a boil and simmer covered for 3½ hours or until meat is fork tender.

Add potatoes, carrots and celery to Dutch oven. Place cabbage on top of meat. Cover and cook for 1 hour or until tender.

Remove vegetables and meat to a large platter. Serve with Horseradish Sauce.

For Horseradish Sauce, melt CRISCO Shortening in a saucepan over medium heat. Stir in flour, salt and pepper. Mix well and cook until bubbly (about 1 minute). Remove from heat. Beat egg yolk; add milk and mix well. Stir into CRISCO mixture. Cook over medium heat, stirring constantly for 3 minutes or until smooth and thickened. Remove from heat. Stir in lemon juice and horseradish.

Spring

St. Pat's Pinwheels

MAKES ABOUT 3 DOZEN COOKIES

1¼ cups sugar

 1 Butter Flavor CRISCO® Stick
   or 1 cup Butter Flavor
   CRISCO Shortening

 2 eggs

¼ cup light corn syrup or
   regular pancake syrup

 1 tablespoon vanilla

 3 cups plus 2 tablespoons
   all-purpose flour, divided

¾ teaspoon baking powder

½ teaspoon baking soda

½ teaspoon salt

½ teaspoon peppermint
   extract

   Green food coloring

Place sugar and CRISCO Shortening in large bowl. Beat at medium speed of electric mixer until well blended. Add eggs, syrup and vanilla; beat until well blended. Combine 3 cups flour, baking powder, baking soda and salt. Add gradually to CRISCO mixture, beating at low speed until well blended.

Place half of dough in medium bowl. Stir in peppermint extract and food coloring, a few drops at a time, until desired shade of green. Shape dough into 2 disks. Wrap with plastic wrap. Refrigerate several hours or until firm.

Sprinkle about 1 tablespoon remaining flour on large sheet of waxed paper. Place peppermint dough on floured paper; flatten slightly with hands. Turn dough over; cover with another large sheet of waxed paper. Roll dough into 14×9-inch rectangle and set aside. Repeat with plain dough.

Remove top sheet of waxed paper from both pieces of dough. Invert plain dough onto peppermint dough, aligning edges carefully. Roll layers together lightly. Remove waxed paper from plain dough. Trim dough to form rectangle. Roll dough tightly in jellyroll fashion starting with long side and using bottom sheet of waxed paper as a guide, removing waxed paper during rolling. Wrap roll in waxed paper; freeze at least 30 minutes or until very firm.

Preheat oven to 375°F.

Place sheets of foil on countertop for cooling cookies. Remove roll from freezer; remove waxed paper. Cut into ⅜-inch-thick slices. Place slices 2 inches apart on ungreased baking sheets.

Bake 1 baking sheet at a time for 7 to 9 minutes or until edges of cookies are very lightly browned. DO NOT OVERBAKE. Cool 2 minutes on baking sheet. Remove cookies to foil to cool completely.

Easter Bunny Cake

MAKES ABOUT 8 SERVINGS

Cake

- 2 egg whites
- 1⅓ cups granulated sugar, divided
- 1¾ cups sifted all-purpose flour
- 1 tablespoon baking powder
- 1 teaspoon salt
- 2 teaspoons vanilla
- 1 cup milk
- ½ cup CRISCO® Oil
- 2 egg yolks

Buttery Cream Frosting

- ½ Butter Flavor CRISCO® Stick or ½ cup Butter Flavor CRISCO Shortening
- 7 cups confectioners' sugar
- 2½ teaspoons vanilla
- ½ cup milk, plus more if needed

  For decorating: flaked coconut, licorice, gumdrops, SMUCKER'S® jelly beans

Preheat oven to 350°F.

Grease and flour 2 (8-inch) round cake pans.

In a large bowl, beat egg whites until soft peaks form.

Gradually add ⅓ cup granulated sugar and continue to beat until peaks are stiff but not dry. Set aside.

In another large bowl combine flour, remaining 1 cup granulated sugar, baking powder and salt. Add vanilla, milk, CRISCO Oil and egg yolks. Mix at medium speed 3 minutes, scraping bottom and sides of bowl often. Fold egg whites into batter until well blended. Pour into pans.

Bake for 20 to 35 minutes or until center springs back when touched lightly and wooden pick inserted in center comes out clean. Cool 20 minutes before removing from pans. Cool completely before frosting.

Buttery Cream Frosting
In medium mixing bowl, beat CRISCO Shortening. Add confectioners' sugar 1 cup at a time. Add vanilla. Slowly blend in milk to desired consistency, adding up to 2 tablespoons more if needed. Beat on high speed for 5 minutes or until smooth and creamy.

Easter Bunny Cake Assembly
Cut ears and bow tie from
1 cake. Arrange whole cake
layer on large serving plate,
with 2 ears positioned at top
and bow tie placed under
the face. Brush off any excess
crumbs; set aside.

Frost entire cake. Sprinkle with
coconut. Arrange thin licorice
strips for whiskers and smile,
gumdrops for eyes and nose
and SMUCKER'S® Jelly Beans
for bow tie decoration.

Herbed Cheese Biscuits

MAKES 12 (2-INCH) BISCUITS

2 cups sifted all-purpose flour

3 teaspoons baking powder

2 teaspoons dried dill

1 teaspoon salt

⅓ CRISCO® Stick or ⅓ cup CRISCO Shortening

½ cup shredded sharp Cheddar or Swiss cheese

¾ cup milk

Preheat oven to 425°F.

In a bowl, mix flour, baking powder, dill and salt. With a pastry blender, 2 knives or a fork, cut in CRISCO Shortening until mixture looks like coarse meal. Stir in shredded cheese. Add milk and stir just until dough holds together.

Place on a lightly floured surface and knead lightly; roll ¾-inch thick. Cut with floured biscuit cutter without turning the biscuit cutter (push straight down) and place on a parchment-lined cookie sheet.

Bake for 12 to 15 minutes or until golden brown.

Recipe Variation
Cinnamon Biscuits: Follow directions for Herbed Cheese Biscuits, omitting cheese and dill. Reduce the milk to ½ cup and sprinkle with a mixture of sugar and cinnamon. Bake at 425°F for 6 to 9 minutes or until golden brown.

Spring

Ham and Cheese Baked Frittata

MAKES 8 SERVINGS

- 6 tablespoons CRISCO® Oil
- 4 cups frozen shredded potatoes or 4 Idaho or russet potatoes, peeled and shredded
- 1½ teaspoons salt, divided
- ½ teaspoon freshly ground black pepper
- 1 pound baked ham, cut into ½-inch cubes
- 12 eggs
- 6 tablespoons milk
- ½ teaspoon Italian seasoning
- 2 cups (8 ounces) shredded Cheddar, Monterey Jack or Swiss cheese
- 1½ cups chunky salsa, heated

Heat oven to 350°F.

Heat CRISCO Oil in 10- or 12-inch skillet on medium heat. Add potatoes. Sprinkle with ½ teaspoon salt and pepper. Cook 8 minutes or until almost brown. Add ham and cook 2 to 3 minutes longer.

Beat eggs with milk, Italian seasoning and remaining 1 teaspoon salt while potatoes are cooking. Place the potatoes into a 9×13-inch casserole sprayed with CRISCO No-Stick Cooking Spray. Stir the egg mixture into the potatoes.

Bake covered for 15 minutes. Remove from oven. Remove cover, sprinkle with cheese and return to the oven. Bake 15 minutes more or until cheese is melted and eggs are set. Turn oven to broil and continue to cook, about 2 minutes or until top is nicely browned. Allow to cool 10 minutes before cutting into 8 squares. Serve topped with heated salsa.

Beef and Bean Chimichangas

MAKES 6 SERVINGS

- 1 pound ground beef
- 2 tablespoons CRISCO® Oil
- 1 medium onion, chopped
- 1 small red bell pepper, diced
- 2 cloves garlic, minced
- 1 can (16 ounces) whole tomatoes, drained and chopped
- ⅓ cup salsa
- 1½ teaspoons chili powder
- ¾ teaspoon ground coriander
- ½ teaspoon dried thyme
- ½ teaspoon salt
- ⅛ teaspoon cayenne
- ⅛ teaspoon ground cumin
- 1 cup refried beans
- 1 cup cooked black beans
- 6 (8-inch) flour tortillas
  CRISCO Oil for frying
- ¾ cup shredded Monterey Jack cheese
  Shredded iceberg lettuce (optional)
  Additional salsa (optional)
  Purchased guacamole (optional)
  Sour cream (optional)

Place ground beef in medium skillet. Brown over medium-high heat. Drain. Remove beef from skillet; set aside. Place 2 tablespoons CRISCO Oil in medium skillet. Add onion, red bell pepper and garlic. Cook and stir over moderate heat until onion is tender. Stir in ground beef, tomatoes, salsa, chili powder, coriander, thyme, salt, cayenne and cumin. Cook over medium-low heat, stirring occasionally, 10 to 15 minutes, or until mixture is thickened. Remove from heat. Stir in refried beans and black beans.

Place ½ cup beef mixture in center of each tortilla. Fold opposite sides of tortilla toward center over beef mixture. Fold ends toward center; secure with wooden pick. Chill 15 minutes.

Heat 2 inches CRISCO Oil in deep-fryer or large saucepan to 375°F.

Fry 1 or 2 chimichangas at a time 1½ to 2 minutes or until golden brown. Drain on paper towels. Sprinkle top of each chimichanga with 2 tablespoons Monterey Jack cheese. Serve immediately on a bed of shredded iceberg lettuce with salsa, guacamole and sour cream, if desired.

Chile Rellenos de Queso (Chiles Stuffed with Cheese)

MAKES 4 SERVINGS

4 poblano chiles*

Filling
- ½ **cup breadcrumbs**
- ½ **cup grated pepper jack cheese**
- ½ **cup grated Cheddar cheese**
- ¼ **teaspoon ground cumin**
- **Salt and black pepper to taste**

Batter
- **CRISCO® Oil for frying**
- 4 **eggs, separated**
- ¼ **teaspoon salt**
- ¼ **cup flour plus additional for sprinkling**

Grated Cheddar cheese

Place chiles on a hot grill or under the broiler; cook until skins are blistered and blackened. Turn occasionally to avoid overcooking and burning. Wrap chiles in a damp cloth or seal in a plastic bag for 20 minutes. The burned skin will peel off easily and the flesh will be slightly cooked by the steam.

Slit the side of each chile, leaving the top of the chile intact. Remove seeds and veins. Rinse chiles and pat dry.

For filling, mix breadcrumbs, cheeses and cumin together; season with salt and pepper. Stuff filling into the slits in the chiles.

Heat at least ¾-inch CRISCO Oil in a heavy, deep pot to 350°F.

For batter, beat egg whites until they are stiff, but not dry. Add salt and egg yolks, 1 at a time, beating well after each addition. Add ¼ cup flour and blend well. Sprinkle chiles lightly with additional flour. Coat chiles with batter.

Preheat oven to 350°F.

Fry chiles in hot oil, turning occasionally, until golden. Drain on paper towels. Sprinkle with Cheddar cheese and melt in oven for 2 to 3 minutes. Serve immediately.

Serve with our **Mexican Rice.**

Chile Rellenos de Queso with Mexican Rice

Mexican Rice

MAKES 4 SERVINGS

2 tablespoons CRISCO® Oil

2 slices bacon, diced

½ medium onion, peeled and chopped

1 rib celery, sliced into 4-inch pieces

2 garlic cloves, peeled and finely chopped

1 cup basmati rice

1½ cups chicken stock

½ cup diced tomatoes with chilies

1 tablespoon sofrito

Salt and black pepper to taste

Heat CRISCO Oil in small sauté pan with a lid. Add diced bacon and cook over medium-high heat until bacon is crisp. Remove bacon, leaving the fat in the skillet. Add the onion, celery and garlic. Cook and stir until the onion is translucent, about 3 minutes, turning the heat down if necessary.

Add rice and stir. Add the chicken stock, tomatoes and sofrito; season with salt and pepper. Bring to a boil; cover and simmer for 20 minutes or until rice is tender. Stir in bacon and serve immediately.

Spring

Miniature Quesadillas

MAKES 4 SERVINGS

- ½ **teaspoon chili powder**
- ½ **teaspoon ground cumin**
- ½ **teaspoon dried oregano leaves**
- ¼ **teaspoon salt**
- 1 **cup shredded Cheddar cheese**
- ½ **cup (about 2 ounces) shredded Monterey Jack cheese**
- 8 **teaspoons CRISCO® Oil, divided**
- 8 **(6-inch) flour tortillas**
- **Fresh salsa (optional)**

Combine chili powder, cumin, oregano and salt in large resealable plastic bag. Add Cheddar and Monterey Jack cheeses. Shake to coat cheese.

Heat 2 teaspoons CRISCO Oil in each of 2 heavy large skillets over medium-high heat. Add 1 tortilla to each skillet. Top each with ¼ cheese mixture. Top each with 1 tortilla. Cook until bottoms are golden brown, about 3 minutes. Turn quesadillas over. Cook until bottoms are golden brown and cheese melts, about 3 minutes.

Transfer to cutting board. Cut each quesadilla into 4 wedges. Transfer to platter. Repeat with remaining CRISCO Oil, tortillas and cheese mixture. Top with salsa, if desired. Serve hot.

Cinco de Mayo

Cinco de Mayo—literally, "the fifth of May"—is a celebration of Mexican identity, unity and patriotism celebrated every spring. The event commemorates the victory of the fledgling Mexican army over more powerful French forces that invaded the country in 1862.

These days, the holiday is celebrated in various regions of Mexico and in many parts of the United States that have large Mexican populations or strong ties to Mexico. It is a great opportunity to celebrate the rich culture and diverse foods of Mexico.

Vanilla Tea Time Cake

MAKES 12 SERVINGS

- **1 Butter Flavor CRISCO® Stick or 1 cup Butter Flavor CRISCO Shortening**
- **2 cups sugar**
- **6 eggs**
- **1 package (12-ounce) vanilla wafers, ground to a coarse meal**
- **½ cup milk**
- **1 can (7½-ounce) sweetened, flaked coconut**
- **1 cup ground pecans**

Preheat oven to 300°F.

Beat together CRISCO Shortening and sugar.

Add eggs 1 at a time, beating well after each addition. Add vanilla wafers and milk. Mix until blended. Add remaining ingredients and mix well.

Thoroughly spray a bundt pan with CRISCO No-Stick Cooking Spray. Dust lightly with flour. Pour batter into pan; bake for 2 hours. Cool in pan on rack for 10 minutes. Run a small sharp knife around the edge of the pan. Invert bundt pan to release cake and cool completely on rack.

Southern Dreams

MAKES 24 SERVINGS

- **1 Butter Flavor CRISCO® Stick or 1 cup Butter Flavor CRISCO Shortening**
- **2 cups packed brown sugar**
- **2 cups all-purpose flour**
- **1 cup pecan pieces**
- **2 eggs, beaten**
- **1 tablespoon almond extract**

Preheat oven to 350°F.

Beat together CRISCO Shortening and sugar. Add flour, pecans, eggs and almond extract. Mix well.

Spray a 9×13-inch baking pan with CRISCO No-Stick Cooking Spray. Spread batter in pan. Bake for 30 to 35 minutes. While still warm, cut cookies into 24 squares.

Vanilla Tea Time Cake ▶

Cherry Nut Coffee Cake

1 (13×9-INCH) COFFEE CAKE

Topping

- ⅓ **cup granulated sugar**
- ¼ **cup all-purpose flour**
- ¼ **Butter Flavor CRISCO® Stick or ¼ cup Butter Flavor CRISCO Shortening**
- ½ **cup sliced almonds or other chopped nuts**

Cake

- ¾ **Butter Flavor CRISCO Stick or ¾ cup Butter Flavor CRISCO Shortening**
- 1¼ **cups granulated sugar**
- 1 **teaspoon vanilla**
- 3 **medium eggs**
- 3 **cups all-purpose flour**
- 1½ **teaspoons baking soda**
- 1 **teaspoon salt**
- 1½ **cups sour cream**
- 1 **can (21 ounces) cherry pie filling**

Glaze

- **Milk**
- 1 **cup confectioners' sugar**
- ½ **teaspoon almond extract**

Preheat oven to 350°F. Spray 13×9-inch pan with Crisco® No-Stick Cooking Spray.

For Topping, combine sugar and flour in small bowl. Mix in CRISCO Shortening until crumbly.

For Cake, beat together CRISCO Shortening, sugar and vanilla in large bowl. Add eggs, beating well. Combine flour, baking soda and salt in medium bowl. Add to CRISCO mixture alternately with sour cream. Spread half the batter in greased pan. Cover with half the cherry pie filling, spreading as evenly as possible. Repeat layers. Sprinkle with nuts and topping mixture.

Bake for 50 minutes or until top is brown and wooden pick inserted in center comes out clean. Cool until slightly warm or to room temperature.

For Glaze, add enough milk (about 1 tablespoon) to confectioners' sugar to make desired consistency. Stir in almond extract. Drizzle over cake.

Quick Raisin Ring

MAKES 1 COFFEECAKE

Ring:

2½ cups Homemade CRISCO® Quick Bread Mix (recipe follows)

½ cup milk

3 tablespoons melted butter, divided

1 cup raisins

⅓ cup packed brown sugar

¼ cup chopped nuts

½ teaspoon ground cinnamon

Glaze:

½ cup confectioners' sugar

1 tablespoon milk

Preheat oven to 375°F.

For Ring, combine CRISCO mix and milk in a bowl, stirring until dry ingredients are moistened.

Roll out dough to a 14×10-inch rectangle on a lightly floured surface. Brush dough with 2 tablespoons melted butter. Combine brown sugar, cinnamon, raisins and nuts; sprinkle over dough. Roll up into a jellyroll. Place sealed-edge-down on a lightly greased cookie sheet. Join ends to form a ring; seal. With scissors, make 12 cuts ⅔ of the way through outer edge of ring at 1-inch intervals. Turn each section on its side. Brush with remaining 1 tablespoon melted butter.

Bake for 25 to 30 minutes or until golden brown.

For Glaze, stir sugar and milk together until smooth. Spoon over hot Quick Raisin Ring.

Homemade CRISCO® Quick Bread Mix

MAKES 12 CUPS MIX

10 cups sifted all-purpose flour

⅓ cup baking powder

¼ cup sugar

1 tablespoon salt

2 CRISCO Sticks or 2 cups CRISCO Shortening

Combine flour, baking powder, sugar and salt in a large bowl. Cut in CRISCO Shortening with pastry blender or 2 knives until mixture resembles coarse meal. Store in covered container up to 6 weeks at room temperature. For longer storage, place in freezer. To measure, spoon mix into measuring cup and level with spatula.

For more great recipes for Homemade CRISCO Quick Bread Mix, visit *www.crisco.com* and click on the recipe tab.

Index

Index